LIFE On
THE CANAL

ANTHONY BURTON

IMPORTANT DATES

1566   Opening of the Exeter Ship Canal, the first to have modern canal locks.

1759   The first Act of Parliament for the building of the Bridgewater Canal, marking the start of the Canal Age.

1766   Work begins on Britain's first canal tunnel on the Trent & Mersey Canal at Harecastle in Staffordshire; it took 11 years to complete.

1787   First iron-hulled canal barge built and launched on the River Severn.

1793   'Canal Mania' year – 21 new canals approved by Parliament.

1802   First experimental steam tug, *Charlotte Dundas*, tried out on the Forth & Clyde Canal.

1812   First commercial steam railway opens at Middleton Colliery, Leeds, offering competition to the canals.

1878   George Smith's book *Our Canal Population* is published, which highlighted social problems among canal families.

1884   An Act of Parliament appoints inspectors to check on overcrowding on boats and school attendance.

1889   The carrying company Fellows, Morton & Clayton begins running steam-powered narrow boats.

1893   Opening of the Manchester Ship Canal.

1904   A school for canal children is opened at the Brentford Boatmen's Institute, just outside London.

1910   A Bolinder diesel engine is fitted into a Thames lighter; the engines were soon installed in many canal boats.

1941   All-women crews are recruited to work canal boats.

1946   Creation of the Inland Waterways Association to help preserve Britain's canal heritage.

1948   The canals are nationalized and control is passed the British Transport Commission.

1964   The Stratford-upon-Avon Canal is reopened, the first success for the canal restoration movement.

2002   Opening of The Falkirk Wheel, a unique rotating boat lift.

2012   Control of Britain's waterways passes to a new charity, the Canal and River Trust.

THE CANAL AGE

In the 18th century it was well known that moving goods by water was far more efficient than doing so by road. On even the best roads, and there were not many of those, a single horse could not pull more than two tons in a wagon, but that same horse could haul 30 tons if it was harnessed to a barge on a river. A huge amount had been done to improve river transport in the early decades of the century, using locks and artificial cuttings to bypass difficult sections of the natural waterway. However, by the middle of the century river improvement had gone as far as it could; there were still whole areas that were a long way from any form of water transport, and these included the new, rapidly developing industrial regions.

The Duke of Bridgewater had coal mines on his estates at Worsley and wanted to sell his coal to Manchester, 6½ miles (10km) away. His first plan was to build a canal to link the mines to the nearby River Irwell, but when the river authorities turned him down he came up with a far bolder idea: he would build his own canal that would be carried across the Irwell on an aqueduct. When the Bridgewater Canal opened in 1761 it created a sensation. People came from miles around to witness the miraculous sight of boats floating over a river, while others were far more impressed by the fact that the price of coal in Manchester was halved. Over the next half-century some 2,000 miles (3,200km) of canal would be built in Britain. The Canal Age had begun.

◄ The Duke of Bridgewater stands proudly before the Barton aqueduct, on the outskirts of Manchester, that carried his pioneering canal across the River Irwell.

BUILDING THE CANALS

Canal construction continued right through to the end of the 1820s, when the focus shifted from waterways to railways. The planning of all the different routes was the responsibility of the Chief Engineers, each of whom had their own individual way of doing things. The first important figure was James Brindley (1716–72), who began his career as engineer for the Bridgewater Canal and found himself in demand for almost all the canal schemes begun over the next few years. His approach was cautious, preferring to go round obstacles rather than through or over them, so that his canals tend to wander across the landscape in great meandering loops, following the natural contours of the land. After Brindley's death a new generation of engineers took over the work, notably William Jessop, Thomas Telford and John Rennie. Their approach was very different,

▲ A rare contemporary illustration of navvies at work, constructing Islington tunnel on the Regent's Canal, London, c.1810.

JAMES BRINDLEY

James Brindley died in 1772, with his greatest work, the Trent & Mersey Canal, still unfinished. His epitaph, published in the *Chester Courant*, began:

> *James Brindley lies amongst these Rocks,*
> *He made Canals, Bridges, and Locks,*
> *To convey Water; he made Tunnels*
> *for Barges, Boats, and Air-Vessels ...*

▲ James Brindley, the first of the great canal engineers; he set the pattern for early canal development.

meeting obstructions head on by using a technique known as 'cut and fill', in which the canals would pierce hills in deep cuttings and the spoil would be used to build up embankments across the valleys.

NAVVIES

It has been customary to speak of canals as being built by named individuals. The Staffs & Worcester was 'built' by Brindley, the Rochdale by Jessop, but they did not do the actual building themselves: that was the job of the tens of thousands of men who worked on canal construction all over Britain. They were known originally as 'navigators' because they

▲ A group photograph of the men who worked to rebuild Blisworth tunnel, in Northamptonshire, on the Grand Union Canal around 1930.

built canal navigations, but that soon became abbreviated to the more familiar 'navvies'. They are as much a part of the story of the life of canals as the boatmen who were to use the waterways.

At first canals were constructed using local labour, but as the men became accustomed to the hard work they found that they could earn more money as professional navvies by moving around the country from canal to canal than they could by returning to their old jobs. It was estimated that an experienced navvy could dig out 12 cubic yards (9 cubic metres) of earth a day – the equivalent of digging a trench 36 feet long, 3 feet wide and 3 feet deep (10m x 1m x 1m).

honours done to his memory, by their numerous and splendid attendance at his funeral.

CANAL NAVIGATIONS, &c.

D. EDSON, Engineer and Architect, having been many years engaged on Canal Navigations in the North of England, has taken up his residence in York-street, Bristol, and solicits the patronage of the Nobility, Gentry, and Public in general, in surveying, estimating and executing Canal Navigations, Roads, Bridges, Sea-Docks, Sea-Banking, and making Pleasure-Ground, with the several Appendages necessary thereto; by whom every Branch of Engineering and Surveying is estimated and executed on eligible Terms.

The best and cheapest ALMANACK extant. This Day is published,

◀ The canals were crucial in developing the new profession of engineering. Dennis Edson advertised his services in a Bristol newspaper in 1792.

➤ Building a canal bridge by laying bricks over a wooden former at Gayton, Northamptonshire, in 1910. The work is almost complete, so a small audience watches as the lady wearing a splendid hat performs the 'topping out' ceremony, laying the final brick.

In 1788 the company that built the Basingstoke Canal tried to employ local men but they proved to be quite incapable of keeping up with the more experienced navvies.

Digging the canal was only part of the navvies' work. In deep cuttings, for example, they had to use barrow runs. The barrow was filled with soil and attached to a horse at the top of the cutting. As the horse walked away, the barrow was pulled up steep planks, with the navvy holding on. It was all too easy for the men to lose their footing on planks covered in greasy clay and end up tumbling down the slope with a barrow-load of earth and rocks falling after them. Among the hardest jobs was 'puddling' – creating a waterproof lining by stomping a gooey mixture of water and clay onto the bed of the canal with the feet. The only aid to manual labour came in tunnelling, when gunpowder was used to blast through the rock. It is astonishing that the whole canal system was constructed with nothing more sophisticated than spade, pickaxe and barrow – and the hardened muscles of thousands of navvies.

THE EARLY YEARS

▲ In the early years it was not unusual for men to bowhaul boats instead of relying on horses as here on the Thames & Severn Canal near Sapperton, Gloucestershire.

There is little evidence regarding the first few years of boating on the canals. What we do know is that boating was much like carting on the roads. Indeed it seems that the first boatmen in the 1770s had been carters: they were the men who knew about looking after horses, and it made very little difference to the horse whether it was pulling a boat or a wagon. It seems that at first no one bothered very much about having someone to steer the boat; it simply bumped its way along the canal, careering into the sides, damaging locks and bridges. Companies eventually put a stop to that, introducing by-laws that decreed that every boat must have someone on board to steer.

No one lived permanently on the boats in these early days. A boatman might have a small cabin in the stern, where he could sleep on long trips, but at the end of a journey he returned to a house, just as a carter or wagoner would have done. Many of the early canals, such as the Birmingham Canal (begun in 1768), were built with a specific trade in mind – in this case to bring coal from the mines of the Black Country into the rapidly developing town of Birmingham itself. The distances were quite short, perhaps no more than a few miles, and all the carrying was done in 'day boats', which were little more than plain hulls. On the Bridgewater Canal it was common to run a string of small boats together for the 5-mile (8-km)

▲ James Brindley's canals typically kept to the natural contours of the land. Here the Oxford Canal winds round the low hill at Wormleighton.

▲ In contrast to the Brindley canals, later engineers took a more direct route. Here Thomas Telford's Shropshire Union Canal slices through a hillside in a deep cutting.

journey from the mines of Worsley Delph to the wharf in Manchester.

CANALS AND RIVERS

As the canal system expanded longer journeys became possible and the disadvantages of the Brindley system became more irksome. The Oxford Canal was part of a vital system, linking the River Thames at Oxford to the Coventry Canal to create a through-route from London to Birmingham. Boatmen became frustrated by the twists and turns of the Oxford Canal. In Warwickshire, at Wormleighton it almost encircled a small hill, and at the northern end of the canal boatmen complained that they could travel all day and still hear the chiming of the church clock at Brinklow. These cross-country routes linked up

with river systems, most of which had a long-established trade involving barges that were unique to specific rivers, such as Mersey flats (flat-bottomed barges) and Severn trows (sailing barges with masts that could be lowered to go under bridges). This meant that there needed to be facilities for changing cargoes from canal boats to riverboats, and at some of these interchange points whole new canal towns developed. Shardlow (where the Trent & Mersey Canal meets the River Trent) and Stourport (at the junction of the Staffs & Worcester Canal) are splendid examples, with Georgian houses surrounding a complex of wharfs and warehouses. The wharfingers who handled cargoes, the chandlers who provided essential supplies, the merchants and their agents all played a vital part in keeping the system working.

◄ Canal tunnels were more than just transport routes. The Dudley Canal tunnel in the West Midlands had side passages that led directly to mines and quarries.

NARROW BOATS

▲ Launching a new narrow boat: they are always launched sideways into the canal.

The Bridgewater Canal was extended in 1762 to reach the River Mersey at Runcorn, and locks were built to take barges that measured roughly 70 feet long by 14 feet wide (20m x 4m) from the Mersey. When Brindley began work on the Trent & Mersey Canal he may well have expected to do the same, but he had an obstacle of a kind he had never faced before: Harecastle Hill, near Stoke-on-Trent, lay right across the line of the route. There was no way round it or over it, so the only option was to go through it in a tunnel that would be over a mile and a half (2.5km) long. He found the idea of building it big enough to take 14-foot (4-m) wide craft too daunting, so he halved the width. And if boats wider than 7 feet (2m) could not go through the tunnel he saw no point in designing locks to take wide boats either. So all the Midland canals were built to take vessels approximately 7 feet (2m) wide by 70 feet (20m) long: the narrow boat was born. Over the years it developed into the familiar form we know today, with most of the hull being used as cargo space and a small cabin at the stern.

BUILDING THE BOATS

The first narrow boats, made in the 1760s, were constructed entirely of wood, though later a combination of wood and iron became more common. Starting at the high bow, protected by a fender, the vessel widens out. The bow area is decked to form a useful storage area below. Behind that, a triangular board, known as the 'cratch', rises above the foredeck. Behind the

◄ A wooden narrow boat under repair. The large wooden tiller at the stern tells us this was designed to be towed by a horse or a motor boat.

BOAT NAMES

Boats and ships have been given names since time immemorial and canal boats were no exception. Individual owners could choose any name that took their fancy, but carrying companies tended to use a theme: the Severn & Canal Carrying Company, for example, named one of their fleets after local rivers – Severn, Avon and Usk.

▲ An artist paints the cabin door of the modestly named *Unostentatious*.

cratch is the cargo hold, basically a flat-bottomed, straight-sided topless box. Wooden planks rise above the hold, stretching from the cratch to the stern cabin. These can be covered with waterproof sheets to protect the cargo. The cabin was added when families began to live on board. At the stern there is the large wooden rudder controlled by a curved wooden tiller, which turns downwards when in use, but can be removed and turned up when the boat is moored to make access to the cabin easier. The other notable feature is a short mast to which the tow rope is attached.

The boats were generally built in small, family-run boatyards. Plans were hardly ever used: the design was kept in the builder's head and passed on from one generation of craftsmen to another. First the planks for the flat bottom were laid out on a trestle. These were usually untreated elm which soaks up water and when saturated lasts for years. Stem and sternposts of oak were then added and sides built up in the space in between. The most common method of getting the side planks to

bend at bow and stern was to steam them to make them flexible. When the hull was complete the seams between the planks were made watertight by cramming in old rope fibres and covering them with tar. When everything was ready the boats were launched sideways into the canal. Finishing touches – such as painting – completed, the narrow boat was ready for its new owner. If you asked a boatman what he thought of his boat, the highest praise he could bestow would be to say 'it swims' – meaning it moves well through the water.

▲ A heavily laden horse-drawn narrow boat on the Coventry Canal. The boatwoman wears traditional costume.

▲ A pair of narrow boats on the Grand Union Canal, passing Bulbourne maintenance yard; the motor boat, with its metal swan-necked till, is towing the unpowered 'butty', with its traditional wooden tiller.

9

WORKING THE BOATS

Anyone who has holidayed on a modern version of the traditional narrow boat may think that the working life on the canals must have been quite idyllic. In fact it represented long hours, hard work and required particular skills.

HORSES

Until the early years of the 20th century, almost every boat on the whole canal system was pulled by a horse, and as a result the horse was uniquely valuable to the boating community. If the animal was ill or injured then all work stopped and no one got paid. Pulling the boat along once it was under way was not a problem, but there was considerable strain involved in getting it started and the horse risked a dislocated shoulder. As there were no vets available, the only cure was to lead it into the canal and hope that swimming would put things right. However, prevention was better than cure and some boatmen used a long tow rope with a pulley system that slipped over a bollard ahead of the horse to help ease the load. Starting was not the only problem. Even when the horse stops the boat keeps on moving, so that

when approaching a lock, for example, the boatman had to use considerable dexterity to loop a line over a bollard to stop his vessel before it crashed into the lock gates.

The horse often got a rest from hauling a loaded boat when it reached a tunnel. Many had no towpath, so the horse had to be unhitched and led over the top to the other end of the tunnel, while the boat was 'legged' through.

LEGGING

The task of 'legging' a boat through a tunnel required two crew members, one on each side of the boat. They lay on their backs, pressed their feet against the tunnel sides and walked the boat through. In wide tunnels, special boards (wings) had to be pushed out from the sides of the boat for the men to lie on so that their feet reached the walls. In some of the longest tunnels professional leggers were employed; one such legger worked out that in his lifetime he had walked a distance equal to the circumference of the earth, while lying on his back.

▲ The horse always had to be well looked after. This one at Banbury lock is enjoying his food and wearing a crocheted hat to protect him from the sun.

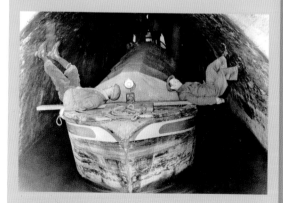

▲ Legging a boat through a tunnel: the men have had to put out 'wings', planks they can lie on in order for their feet to reach the sides of the tunnel.

Boatwomen unloading coal from a narrow boat at Juxon Street wharf on the Oxford Canal. They are nearing the bottom of the boat so the coal has to be thrown shoulder high.

A boatman managing the tow rope on one of Samuel Barlow's coal boats. The rope work round the top of the tiller and the painted roses and castles are typical traditional boat decorations.

LOCKS

Locks presented a problem of quite a different nature. It was a matter of pride among a boating community that they could work through locks with great efficiency and as quickly as possible. The shorter the journey time in delivering a cargo, the sooner the boatman got paid and could take on the next load. But on a busy canal, although there were regulations over who should have the right of way in approaching a lock, in practice it was not unknown for arguments to break out and sometimes matters were settled in a fight.

LOADING AND UNLOADING

Moving the boats was only a part of the story. The boaters were generally also responsible for loading and unloading the cargo. Coal was one of the most common cargoes, and while loading it into the boat was very straightforward, shovelling it out was a very different matter. The more you shovelled out, the harder the work became as you had to throw the coal ever higher to clear the sides of the boat and get it onto the wharf.

Even at the end of the day there was no immediate rest. A hot meal might be beckoning or a pint waiting at a canal-side pub, but before they could be enjoyed there was one other chore to perform. The horse had to be fed, watered and bedded down for the night.

Canal boat people were generally healthy but when they eventually suffered the fate of all humanity and died they were often given lavish funerals. Here the coffin lies in a flower-decked narrow boat.

CARGO AND CARRIERS

▲ Loading a mixed cargo onto a narrow boat at the Albion Basin in Birmingham, where goods were interchanged between the canal and the London Midland Railway.

It is possible to establish the sort of goods the canal companies expected to carry from the tolls they charged, as laid down in the Act of Parliament that authorized construction. Some tolls were very simple: the Trent & Mersey Canal had just one rate covering everything, but others were much more specific. The Pocklington Canal split their rates into 25 different categories, each with its own rate, one of which listed 'boxes, cloth, coffee, dying woods, dry goods, fruit in chests or boxes, glass groceries, hides, hops, paint, parcels, rice, saltpetre, spirits, starch, sumach, tar, tin, turpentine, wines, welds and yarn'. In other words the boats could carry just about anything, but for those who did the carrying the nature of the cargo made a huge difference. The one cargo

everyone hated was grain, simply because it created clouds of choking dust, and if it got too hot and damp it started to germinate and began to smell: no amount of scrubbing would get rid of the stench for weeks. On the other hand delivering chocolate crumb – a dried mixture of sugar, milk and cocoa solids – to the Cadbury factory on the Worcester & Birmingham Canal was very popular with crews who had a sweet tooth. One boatman, Charlie Atkins, had the trade on a regular basis, and was universally known as 'Chocolate Charlie'.

COMPANY FLEETS
Very few canal companies ran their own boats, but over the years a number of companies emerged who had large fleets. Among the first was a firm

▲ Many companies established premises right next to the canal to make the maximum use of cheap transport. This is the Eagle Foundry in Leamington Spa, Warwickshire.

OLD CROMPTON'S RICHES

Few boatmen made much money, but one managed to do so. In the 1920s a 'Number One' known as 'Old Crompton' was involved in an accident when a crane dropped a load into his boat and sank it in a deep dock. The injured man kept repeating 'bed, bed' – but, assuming he wanted to rest, no one could get him to go to bed. Eventually divers went down and brought up his bed – and Old Crompton's anxiety was explained. In the drawer of the bed were one hundred gold sovereigns.

that had begun by carrying goods by road, then switched to the canals – and are again known today as road hauliers: Pickfords. They ran boats between London and Manchester and were famous for their fly boats, so-called because they worked day and night, using relays of horses and change crews. A boat leaving Braunston in Northamptonshire on one morning, for example, would be in Leicester early the next day, having covered over 46 miles (74km), passed through 47 locks and negotiated three tunnels – all without the benefit of an engine.

'NUMBER ONES'

There were also families who preferred to run their own boats, picking up whatever cargoes they could find. Known as 'Number Ones', theirs was a hard life but often one that they valued for its sense of independence. Joe Skinner and his

wife Rose were the very last to carry on trading in this way. When Joe died in 1975, Rose had a home 'on the land' as it was known, but she never really settled there. Every day she would go down to their old boat, *Friendship*, that was moored at Hawkesbury Junction, where the Oxford and Coventry canals meet. She was always ready to greet visitors with a cup of tea and show them old photographs of Joe and his mules – he always preferred them to horses. After Rose died in 1976, *Friendship* found a new home, given a place of honour in the canal museum at Ellesmere Port.

RESOLVED AND ORDERED—
That the Owner or Person in charge of any Boat, Barge, or other Vessel, not having any Horse on the spot to haul the same, who shall attempt to pass into any Lock on the said Canal until any other Boat then in sight, furnished with a Horse or with Steam Power, shall have passed, shall forfeit and pay for every such Offence the sum of FIVE POUNDS.

RESOLVED AND ORDERED—
That every Boat or Barge shall give way to every Boat commonly called a Fly Boat, and navigated by relays of Horses or Steam Power on this Canal, or the Cuts therefrom, on pain that the Master or Person having the command of such Boat or Barge, and refusing or not allowing any Fly Boat to pass, shall forfeit and pay the sum of TWENTY SHILLINGS.

CHARLES ROGERS,

▲ Grand Junction rules, including giving priority to fly boats.

◄ The Severn & Canal Carrying Company ran fleets of motorized barges and narrow boats; the latter were often towed in large numbers down the River Severn by tugs.

THE MAINTENANCE MEN

Like all transport systems canals need regular maintenance to keep everything in good working order, and the workers responsible were an important part of the canal community. Canal maintenance yards were at the heart of the operation. Most had workshops where they could make such essentials as lock gates, which had to be replaced at regular intervals, and there would also be a forge to look after ironwork, such as paddle gear: they could make just about anything that was needed to keep the system running.

DRAINING

Work while out on the canal presented its own difficulties. A lot of jobs could only be carried out by draining the waterway. All along the route there would be 'stop planks' that could be slipped into grooves in the canal sides to make temporary dams. There were various ways of emptying the canal in the days before electric pumps came into use. In some canals, built in porous ground, there were plugs that could be pulled so that it emptied like a bathtub; otherwise hand-operated pumps were the usual answer.

DREDGING

Other work could be carried out without draining. Dredging was a constant requirement to keep the channel open, and was hard work. In the early days this task was usually carried out by a 'bag and spoon' dredger. The spoon was a metal ring, usually 2–3 feet (0.6–1m) in diameter, to which a large leather bag was attached. It was fastened on the end of a long pole that was dropped over the side of the maintenance boat to scoop up the mud as the boat was pulled along. The hard work came when it had to be hauled up, full of slime, then emptied.

PILE DRIVING

To protect the bank, rows of solid wooden or metal posts (piles) were driven into the ground at the water's edge. Pile driving usually involved raising a heavy weight using a pulley system and then letting it drop onto the pile, to force it down. Bank protection was vital, but not always successful. Many canals, such as the Brecon &

▲ A new lock gate being lowered into place using shearlegs. Similar methods would have been used when canals were first built.

> ➤ What happens when things go wrong: this embankment collapsed on the canal near Llangollen, North Wales, in 1960, resulting in a long period of closure.

> ◄ Making a new balance beam, using traditional tools. The men are working with a two-handed saw, and the beam has been shaped by an adze, seen in the foreground.

> ➤ Pile driving on the Grand Union Canal. The pile driver is lifted by the pulley and then allowed to drop onto the piles, thus serving to protect the bank from erosion.

Abergavenny, were built into the sides of hills and were always susceptible to landslips, especially after heavy rain. When that happened there was nothing to be done but to close the canal and build everything up again.

ICE BREAKERS

There was another problem that was likely to happen on an annual basis – ice. It could freeze

lock gates together, so that they had to be chipped clear before they could be used, but in a really severe winter the canal itself could freeze over. Then the ice breaker was brought out. This was a boat with a specially reinforced hull, and a tall rail down the centre. The towing horse would get up a good gallop and haul the breaker at speed towards the ice. Once the boat was run up onto the ice, the men on board would hold onto the rail and begin rocking it vigorously from side to side. The process did not always work, and when it failed the canal boats could be stuck fast and the families, with no money coming in, could be reduced to begging in the local towns.

There was nothing romantic about the life of the maintenance gangs, but their work was vital for the running of the whole system.

> ◄ When the canal completely froze in 1895 and all carrying stopped, these boatmen were forced to go into Worcester with their model narrow boat to beg for funds.

THE LOCK KEEPER

◄ Junction House, Kings Norton, in the West Midlands: this elegant house was built in 1796 to serve as both the offices and tollhouse for the Worcester & Birmingham Canal Company.

▼ A lock keeper in the 19th century, taking a rest on a bollard.

As well as a maintenance force, the canal companies who owned the waterways – like any other commercial concern – needed offices for administration, often housed in quite grand buildings. The offices of the Kennet & Avon Canal in Bath, for example, were housed in a handsome building, built on a bridge over the canal, that fits in perfectly with the surrounding Georgian architecture. The general secretary was in charge, helped by the usual staff consisting of clerks and book-keepers. But the main work of the canal was carried out in far humbler offices, spread up and down the whole system.

Lock keepers generally lived rent-free in cottages provided by the company. The one thing they did not do was open and close locks, though they were responsible for seeing that they were properly used. As engineer John Smeaton explained in his instructions, they were to stop the boatmen 'running against the lock-gates, leaving the cloughs [sluices] running, so as to let off the water etc'.

Maintaining water levels throughout the system was a vital part of a lock keeper's work. Some canals did not allow locks to be used at night. A lock keeper at Bingley on the Leeds & Liverpool Canal rigged up an ingenious arrangement of tripwires and bells to warn him of any offenders. The boatmen got round that – they paid a succession of local lads to ring the bells through the night. The system was soon abandoned.

An island tollhouse on a quiet day on the main line of the Birmingham Canal. Boats would be tied up to be gauged, and the amount of tolls they had to pay calculated.

◄ Cropredy lock on the Oxford Canal in the middle of the 20th century. Most lock keepers were proud of their cottages and kept attractive gardens at the waterside.

TOLLS

Toll collection was sometimes left to special collectors who had their own offices, but on some canals it was also part of the lock keeper's job. Tolls were based on how canal boats were gauged. Before the boats went into service, they were loaded with different weights and the height of the water at the side of the boat was marked for the different loads. The toll collector had a gauging rod which he put against the mark to read off how much cargo was being carried. The boatmen who wanted to cut their costs had various tricks of the trade. When the gauging rod was being applied, they would suddenly see a friend on the opposite bank and lean over the side of the boat – raising the side that was being measured. Different cargoes were charged at different rates, so the more expensive goods might be hidden away under a cheaper produce, in the hope the collector would only spot the cheaper goods on top.

The lock keepers were not well paid, but they did have security and generally the companies looked after them well. When the Cropredy keeper on the Oxford Canal died in the 1850s his widow was allowed to take over the job and was still officially in charge until she was 74.

BANBURY LOCK

Rose MacDonald had happy memories of being brought up during the 1930s in the cottage at Banbury lock on the Oxford Canal, where her father collected tolls: 'Very cosy inside, a desk right across the window where he perched on a high stool to write in the big ledger. Two armchairs, one was his, and one for the current dog and probably one of us children, or one of his cronies, a cosy coal fire in cold weather … my brightest memories of him are those of him skipping as lively across the boats, with his gauge over his arm, notebook and pencil at the ready.'

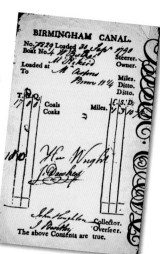

➤ A toll ticket of 1790 showing that a boat loaded with 17 tons of coal had travelled 11¼ miles (18.1km) and had to pay a fee of £1 3s 10d (£1.19).

THE BACK CABIN

The opening of the railway between Liverpool and Manchester in 1830 marked the start of a huge expansion of the rail network. The only way the canals could compete with this new, fast service was to cut costs and one way to do that was for boatmen to abandon their houses and cottages and live permanently on the boats, bringing their families with them.

Nothing could be done to increase the size of the canal narrow boat, as anything bigger would be unable to get through a lock. So as most of the space had to be taken up with the cargo hold, all that was left for the families was a cabin approximately 8½ feet long, 7 feet wide and 5 feet high (2.5m x 2m x 1.5m). To fit a married couple, their children and all the family possessions into such a space was a miracle of organization. The main piece of furniture was a large cupboard, the front of which folded down to make a bed, though it was hardly king-size, being little more than 6 feet long and 3 feet 3 inches across (1.8m x 1m). A second cupboard contained the food, and it too had a drop-down front that was used as a table. There was a side bed for the children. The other important item was the range for heating and cooking.

▲ Wash day on a narrow boat usually involved nothing more complicated than a galvanized tub in the bows and water from the canal.

MAKING THE BEST OF IT

The families did their best to make this constricted space as comfortable and cosy as possible. Brasswork was polished, the range blacked and decorative items, especially lace-edged plates, were hung on the cabin walls. The most important decoration was the painting of traditional roses and castles on the cabin and its cupboard doors. No one is certain how the tradition developed; some have suggested that it derives from Romany

▲ Teatime in the back cabin; from the *Illustrated London News*, 1874.

WHAT'S FOR DINNER?

In 1920 the manager of the Shropshire Union Company fleet recorded that the food stores of the boat families consisted mainly of beef, bacon, cheese and butter. Many supplemented their supplies by setting snares for rabbits, and even scooped mallard out of the canal. The boatmen often referred to arable farmland as their 'back garden'. Fresh milk tended to be a problem and in later years sterilized milk became popular – or 'paralysed milk' as one boy always called it.

▲ Painting roses and castles. This was a very specialized craft, and the different painters all had their own distinctive styles.

▲ Charlie Carter collecting drinking water at Hawkesbury Junction, a popular meeting place for boat families. He is filling traditionally decorated Buckby cans.

caravans, but the style of decoration is quite different. Perhaps the families were looking back to the days when they had their own cottages and gardens. If they could not live in an actual castle at least they could live amongst painted pictures of them, and enjoy painted roses instead of the real thing.

The boats had no amenities of any kind. Water had to be fetched from a tap or pump using a decorated Buckby can kept on the cabin roof. Washing of people and clothes often depended on using canal water, and of course there were no toilet facilities of any kind. E. Thurston Dart, who took a trip on a narrow boat in 1913, asked the boatman, Henry, what the families did. 'Why, look you, sur,' he replied, 'that hedge which runs along by every towpath. If Nature couldn't grow enough leaves on that hedge to hide a sparrow's nest, it ain't no good to God, man, nor beast.' Most of us would find it impossible to live in such cramped conditions today, but as one elderly boatwoman looking back on her life said, 'If I had my choice again I would do it all again exactly the same.'

BUCKBY CANS

These cans were used to hold fresh water, and they could hold as much as 3 gallons (11 litres) each. The cans always had a lid, and provided a useful stepping stone for getting off the cabin roof to reach the side of a lock. No one seems quite certain where the name originates, but one of the places they were sold was Long Buckby on the Grand Union Canal.

▲ Decorating a Buckby can in traditional style.

CANAL CHILDREN

▼ A family group posing for a photograph at Stoke Bruerne, Northamptonshire, on the Grand Union Canal in the early 20th century. They probably all squeezed into one boat.

Looking after children on the boats was always a problem. When they were very young they were usually put in a harness and secured to the boat, but as they grew they were soon free to clamber around. The one exception was in tunnels, when they were shut in the back cabin, and no amount of pleading would get them out: 'Let's come out mam, let's come out mam – and mam kicked us back in.' But the years of playing on the boat were short lived. The children were soon put to work.

One of the first jobs children were given was 'lock wheeling', going ahead of the boat to get a lock ready. One boatman remembers cycling ahead, when his bike hit a rut and shot him into the canal. He could not swim, but as the boat came past his mother grabbed him by his hair and deposited him on the bank before continuing on

her way. Older children spent a lot of time leading the horses, and were often given the job of taking the horse over the tunnel while a boat was legged through. Nell Cartwright, a child in Edwardian

▲ The floating boatmen's chapel, a converted houseboat, moored on the River Thames at Oxford, alongside the canal towpath.

▲ Sister Mary Ward was a well-known character at Stoke Bruerne, where she ministered to the basic medical needs of generations of boat families.

▲ Children wait for their parents on a narrow boat at Chirk on the Llangollen Canal. The rails are from a tramway, which brought freight to the canal in horse-drawn wagons.

times, was only 13 when she had to take the horse over the top of the long Braunston tunnel on a dark night. She was terrified at first, but the horse kept nuzzling her: 'I thought to myself, "He's telling me not to be afraid", and when I got to the end of the tunnel I was brave as brave.'

Bob Bunn remembers that, as an 8-year-old, he walked the 93 miles (150km) of the Grand Union from Brentford to Braunston, opening and closing all the lock gates, and got paid sixpence (2½p). Children learned to handle the boats at a young age as well, and one lad was given his own boat when he was just 14.

AN EDUCATION

One thing was inevitably missing from their lives: there was no education for boat children in the 19th century – and very little concern for their welfare. There were a few attempts to improve matters. Henry Ward of Oxford converted a houseboat into a floating chapel and schoolroom. Another man who took an active interest was George Smith, a philanthropist whose book *Our Canal Population*, published in 1878, brought conditions on the canal to a wider public. He discovered that 90 per cent of the children were illiterate and that, in spite of the efforts of men like Henry Ward, most were 'utterly ignorant of all religious knowledge'. Smith began campaigning to improve their lives. The result was an Act of Parliament passed in 1884 that enforced attendance at school and allowed inspection of boats to prevent gross overcrowding. Each child had an attendance book that had to be signed by a teacher when they arrived at school: what it did not show

was that all too often the child had scarcely sat down before mother arrived to say they were moving on. As far as officialdom was concerned that attendance book was marked so all was well. Education only really improved when a special school for boat children was opened at Brentford, just outside London, in the early 1900s.

FLOATING SCHOOL

The floating school at Brentford provided an educational opportunity but it was not perfect. A report in *The Times* in the 1930s noted: 'Considering the difficulties, the attainments of the children are reasonably good … but it is impossible that they should be equal to those of children of the same age in regular attendance at schools.' Learning to read was the main obstacle. One boatwoman recorded how she had learned her alphabet from the letters on goods wagons on the canalside railway.

▲ Boat children at the floating school established for them at Brentford. Education had to be fitted in while the boats were moored for loading and unloading.

PASSENGER BOATS

The Duke of Bridgewater began running fare-paying passenger boats (packet boats) as early as 1772. The boats had three classes and passengers had a choice of staying in the cabin or taking a seat on the cabin roof. Refreshments were provided, including alcoholic drinks. Sir George Head described a trip in his book *A Home Tour Through the Manufacturing Districts of England* (1835): he was alarmed when a lady passenger fell off the roof and rushed to help, but 'as I picked her up, she let forth a sigh, which smelt so strongly of rum that I was happy to consign her collapsed form into other hands'. Soon similar packet boats were operating on many canals, and as they were running to a regular timetable they were given priority over other craft. The Bridgewater Canal packets had a unique way of ensuring no one got in their way: they had a sickle blade in the bow that cut through the tow rope of any vessel that refused to let them through.

Market boats carried produce rather than passengers, but poorer people could usually get a ride for just a few pence, even if they had to perch on top of sacks for the journey. In 1839 a young woman called Christine Collins got a lift on a Pickfords boat heading for Liverpool. She never arrived: she was murdered and her body dumped in the canal. This was a unique tragedy: tens of thousands took similar trips without coming to any harm at all.

FACING THE COMPETITION

The arrival of the railways brought severe competition to canal travel and a new generation of speedy boats was developed, known as 'Scotch' or 'swift' boats. The first, developed for use on the Glasgow, Paisley & Johnstone Canal, were 60 feet (18m) in length, but only 4½ feet (1.3m) beam (width), though they were later extended to 6 foot beam (1.8m). They were drawn by teams of two

▲ A packet boat that operated on the Grand Junction, now the Grand Union, Canal between Paddington Basin and Uxbridge, Middlesex, at the beginning of the 19th century.

▲ Crowded pleasure steamers on the Forth & Clyde Canal. Thanks to a 21st-century restoration programme, such boats are once again running on this canal.

WE ARE AMUSED

Scottish canals were the first to introduce steamers for passengers and they received the royal seal of approval in 1873 when Queen Victoria took a trip on the Caledonian Canal steamer *Gondolier*. She found the journey 'tedious', but was entertained by the locks: 'It was amusing to see the people, including the crew of the steamer, who went on shore to expedite the operation, run round and round to move the windlasses.'

▲ The slender Lancaster Canal swift, designed to be pulled at speed by a team of galloping horses.

or three horses managed by liveried postilions and could achieve speeds of 12mph (19kph), with regular changes of horses. Sir George Head continued his canal travels in Scotland on a swift: 'She was to all appearances so cranky – toppling and rolling from side to side so awfully when empty, that people took a panic, and many declined on any account to venture.' Those who did venture found that once under way the boat moved smoothly through the water, and they could enjoy a luxurious cabin equipped with comfortable chairs, books to read, a fire in winter and good food and wine.

PLEASURE BOATS

A new form of passenger travel began to develop at the end of the 19th century. As early as 1873 two young ladies hired a narrow boat and crew to take them on a canal holiday, though first they had

to make appropriate alterations by panelling the inside of the hull and fitting it out, reporting: 'There were curtains to be hung, Liberty curtains that had taken a whole day to choose, and "dhurries" [rugs] to be draped over the fresh-scented pine of the little cabins; and Liberty again in innumerable hangings to be arranged all round the bulwarks gracefully.' Not many followed their pioneering efforts initially, but short trips by pleasure boat on the more scenic canals became increasingly popular, leading the way towards the pleasure boating of today.

➤ Lancaster Canal passenger boat timetable.

▼ Passengers waiting for the horse to be hitched up to their boat at Llangollen. This same service is still being run today, a century later.

BROAD BOATS FOR WIDE WATERWAYS

Although the narrow boat is seen as the quintessential canal craft, it was by no means the only type of vessel using the canal system. Long before the first purely artificial canals were constructed, a large variety of barges were in use on the rivers and some of these would also be able to travel on the wide canals. The locks on the Stroudwater Canal in Gloucestershire, for example, were specifically designed to take the trows of the River Severn. These craft were able to work in the Severn estuary down as far as the ports of South Wales, as well as serving the woollen mills of the Stroud valleys.

The Humber keels, by contrast, were very basic. Very bluff (wide) at bow and stern, with a hull shaped rather like a date box, they carried two square sails on a single mast. As their name suggests, they were originally used on the Humber and Trent rivers, but in later years they travelled inland as far as Sheffield.

Not all broad-beamed vessels had sails; on canals such as the Leeds & Liverpool, the boats were hauled by horses just as narrow boats were.

CLYDE PUFFERS

Scottish canals were also wide waterways and they too developed their own individual types of craft. The best known is the 'Clyde puffer', built originally for use on the Forth & Clyde Canal. These are steamers that got their name because, in the first versions, the exhaust steam went up the chimney, producing little puffs of smoke.

◄ Wide boats stuck fast in the ice on the Rochdale Canal. Travelling on this canal was hard work, with 92 locks in just 33 miles (53km).

◄ A Humber keel under sail on the Stainforth & Keadby Canal, part of the Sheffield and South Yorkshire Navigation. The 'barge boards' at the side of the hull could be let down into the water to act as a keel when working in the Humber estuary.

∧ A Clyde puffer being loaded with barrels of whisky at Port Dundas on the Forth & Clyde Canal. These versatile craft also served the islands off Scotland's west coast.

They achieved fame through Neil Munro's *Para Handy* stories. Para Handy was skipper of the *Vital Spark*, a workaday vessel to all but her proud owner: 'Oh Man! She was chust sublime! She should be carryin' nothing but gentry for passengers.' One of these fine craft, the *VIC 32*, still steams along the canals and round the west coast of Scotland, helping to preserve something of the rich variety of canal and river craft.

A LIFETIME ON THE CANAL

Fred Schofield was born in 1906 and took his first trip on the canal with his father when he was only three weeks old. Although they had a house, the family often went on board for several days at a time. He said, 'Mother would be busy a day or two before the ship was expected, making ready for closing the house, and getting all the washing out of the way. She also tried to have a good baking day.' Once aboard, his mother not only looked after all the cooking, but also acted as mate.

Fred learned how to handle the craft as he grew up, and by the age of 13 he was working full-time for his father. If there was no wind to fill the sails on a canal they had to hire horses to pull the vessel along, looked after by men known as the 'horse marines'. When he finally retired, his last keel, *Comrade*, was sold to the Humber Keel and Sloop Preservation Trust and still regularly sails the River Humber. Fred taught the members how to sail his old craft but, as he said, good as they were they would never really know what it was like to work the vessel in all conditions and all seasons as he had done.

POWER ON THE CANALS

Perhaps one of the more surprising things about life on the canals is that for most of their working life boats were still being pulled by horses, while steam locomotives hauled trains, and traction engines appeared on the road. There were early experiments, however, to power canal boats. William Symington, a Scottish engineer, was fascinated by steam; he put an engine in a pleasure boat near Dumfries and took the poet Robert Burns along for the ride. He followed this by building a steam tug and in 1803 it successfully pulled two fully laden 70-ton barges along the Forth & Clyde Canal. But the proprietors were worried about the wash damaging the banks and the whole scheme was abandoned.

STEAMERS

Later in the 19th century, steam tugs became more widely used. They were particularly useful in hauling narrow boats through tunnels, to the delight of the boatmen who no longer had the tedious job of legging them through. The first steam narrow boats were built in the 1860s. From 1889, the carrying company Fellows, Morton & Clayton built up a fleet of 31 steamers. However, there was a problem with the steamers: the engine and coal bunker took up a lot of space that had previously been used for cargo, but they could haul a second boat along behind them. Even so, in order to make them pay the company had to run them as fly boats, working day and night. There was usually a crew of five on the steamer and three on the second boat, all kitted out in smart white uniforms. The other problem was communication: the steerer could not control

▲ Tickets for tug towing.

◄ One of the large fleet of steamers run by Fellows, Morton & Clayton. The engineer is leaning out in the gap between the cabin and his engine house.

HORSES OR MOTORS?

Most regarded the introduction of motors on canal boats as a great boon — but not everyone. Nell Cartwright, interviewed as an old lady in 1977, was less keen. 'I liked my horse and I liked the boat as it was,' she said. 'When they brought the noisy motors I didn't like that at all. They frightened me because I don't think it was so peaceful and there was no beauty. I mean you look along the boat as it was going and you see that horse just walking along the road and the hedges and trees and everything going by. No one could ask for better than that.'

▲ A motor boat, one of the fleet run by Ovaltine to supply their West Midlands factory, towing its butty through a bridge on the Grand Union Canal.

▲ Horses stand on the bank as boats wait to be towed through Blisworth tunnel on the Grand Junction Canal in 1910. The steam tug can be seen in the bottom left-hand corner.

the engine, the engine driver could not see where they were going, and their only means of communication was by tugging on a lanyard.

THE HOT-BULB ENGINE

The big change came when a Swedish engineer, Erik August Bolinder, designed a two-stroke diesel engine. It was a hot-bulb engine: in other words in order to get it going the fuel had to be heated in a vaporizer using a blowlamp. The boating community were more than a little alarmed by the idea, and subsequently the Bolinder salesmen had a special demonstration: they poured some diesel into the hold and threw in a lighted match. The fuel never ignited. Acceptance was slow but by 1930 over 200 narrow boats had been fitted out with the engines, and the 'pop-pop' of a Bolinder became as familiar a sound on the canals as the clatter of hoofs had once been.

Now a family could run two boats, a motorboat and a 'butty' (an unpowered boat) towed behind it. Not only could they carry more cargo, but they now had two cabins to house the family.

▲ A Thames & Severn tug hauling a string of narrow boats out of Gloucester Docks on their way to the Gloucester & Sharpness Canal.

'IDLE WOMEN'

The name 'Idle Women' was given to the females who volunteered for canal work during the Second World War. It was a joke based on the fact that they had badges with the initials IW, which in fact simply stood for Inland Waterways. One thing they were not was idle.

Many of the women joined up because they had enjoyed messing about in boats as children, but they were to find that working a narrow boat had very little in common with yachting on The Broads. They were given basic training in boat handling by Kit Gayford and Daphne French, and then were sent on their way, mostly working on the Grand Union Canal. Even when they had finished their instruction, the women were still known as trainees. It was decided that rather than work with existing crews, they would form their own all-volunteer crews. They found it difficult at first to fit in with the traditional boating families, who regarded them with initial suspicion. 'For the most part the boaters took it stoically,' wrote one of the women, Emma Smith. 'They watched narrowly, in silence, and they spat and they waited.'

EARNING RESPECT

The women knew it was up to them to prove they could do the job and to stand up for themselves. In her book *Idle Women,* Susan Woolfit told of an incident when her crew had just got a lock ready,

◄ Two of the 'Idle Women' working as crew for a Grand Union Canal Carrying Company boat. One of them is poling the boat away from the bank.

◄ Instructor Kit Gayford, wearing her trademark ear-flapped cap, takes a group of trainees along a towpath during the Second World War.

⋀ The canals were not necessarily safe places to work during the war years; the lock at Banbury on the Oxford Canal was hit by a bomb.

but before they could move the boats in another pair of boats tried to force their way in ahead of them. There followed a slanging match in which they 'touched on the doubtful domestic habit of one another's forebears' but in the end the women gave way and had to follow the men up the 21 locks at Hatton, Warwickshire. They had their revenge when they later found one of the same boats stuck firmly in the mud, and the men had to suffer the indignity of being hauled off by the trainees. After that the two crews became firm friends. As Susan Woolfit explained, they had earned respect both by fighting for their rights in the first place and by not bearing a grudge afterwards.

The work was hard and not without its dangers. Many of the trips started at Brentford, on the edge of London, but the women were often required to pick up cargoes at Limehouse Dock, a prime target for German bombers. Susan Woolfit was in the back cabin when a V-2 rocket

hit a factory next to the wharf, and though she was unscathed the boat was badly knocked about.

In time the women were accepted into the boating community, and it was generally agreed that they worked as hard as anyone and, as some boat-women caustically commented, a good deal harder than their husbands. When the war ended, the vast majority went back to their old lives.

SONIA ROLT

One of the 'Idle Women', Sonia South, had originally trained as an actress. After the war she chose not to go back to her old life following her time as a volunteer; she stayed on the canals and married boatman George Smith. It did not last, though they remained good friends, and she kept her connections with the waterways as she was married again, to L.T.C. (Tom) Rolt. Tom Rolt (1910–74) led the movement towards preserving the waterways heritage and in 1946 helped found the Inland Waterways Association (IWA), of which Sonia was an early member.

END OF THE CANAL AGE

The decline in canal carrying really began with the growth of the railway network. A number of canals were actually bought up by railway companies, and though they were required by Act of Parliament to keep them open, there was nothing that said they had to do anything more. Repairs were neglected and when they were carried out the work was slow, causing long closures. A Parliamentary Committee of 1883 found that tolls on railway-owned canals were five times those on the independent canals, as a result of which traffic fell away as old customers did what the railways wanted – sent their goods by rail. All the canals could do was try to offer competitive prices, which usually involved the boating families working longer hours for less pay.

A NEW THREAT

In spite of these difficulties many canals did well throughout the 19th century, but a much greater threat appeared immediately after the First World War. In 1920 the Ministry of Munitions sold off around 20,000 war-surplus trucks at knock-down prices. The new owners were subject to few regulations, had no need to pay tolls on the goods they carried and could offer a reasonably fast door-to-door service. On top of this, in order to get their businesses started they were prepared to work long hours, do all their own maintenance and cut their prices to a minimum. The canal companies responded by amalgamating and modernizing, building new locks on those canals where trade was brisk. The through-route from

▼ Canal officials consider what to do next when confronted by striking boatmen at Braunston in 1923. The men were objecting to a reduction in pay.

By the second half of the 20th century commercial carrying had virtually ended on the narrow waterways, and many boats were left to rot.

THE GRAND UNION CANAL

The Grand Union Canal formed the main-line route between London and Birmingham. It had numerous tributaries, including a main link to Leicester. Major improvements to the old system started in 1932, when the GUCC began replacing the narrow locks between Birmingham and Braunston with 51 new broad locks, each able to take two narrow boats side by side. The company also began running its own fleet of boats as the Grand Union Canal Carrying Company Ltd.

London to Birmingham, for example, had involved journeys on five different canals: now these were joined together to form the Grand Union Canal Company (GUCC). The carriers tried to cut their costs and the easiest way to do that was to pay the crews less. Fellows, Morton & Clayton (FMC) led the way and the result was the first-ever strike by boat crews in 1923. FMC crews all gathered at Braunston and chained their boats together to prevent them being used: the company sent men under police escort to cut them free. There was a fight, after which the boats remained chained. The strike lasted for 17 weeks, and the men claimed a victory. But the underlying problem never went away.

THE STORY CONTINUES

There was a reprieve for the canals when they carried essential goods during the Second World War and when it ended they were taken over as part of the new nationalized transport system. A survey showed that less than half the canals were making a profit and many were making big losses. It was decided to concentrate on the profitable canals and close many more. But even boating families working on canals such as the Grand Union began to leave the industry. As one family explained, they loved the life but they had to think of the future for their children: they would need the sort of education that the nomadic life on the boats could never provide.

After nationalization in 1948, the carrying fleets were mostly taken over by British Waterways. Here a pair of their boats is leaving a lock on the Grand Union Canal.

Commercial carrying on most of the canals was coming to a close in the 1950s, but it was not the end of the story. A new movement grew up that would restore old waterways and open them up – not for cargo but for pleasure boats, helping to create the canal world we know today. And the work still goes on: all over the country workers are busy bringing old, disused canals back to life. Cargo-carrying days may be over, but there are probably more boats on our canals today than there have ever been in the last 250 years. And as recently as 2012, a new charity – the Canal and River Trust (www.canalrivertrust.org.uk) – was formed, heralding a new era in the preservation of our waterways for generations to come.

The museums and heritage centres listed below all provide insights into the history of the canal network. Contact the sites or visit their websites for further information including details of opening times.

The Black Country Living Museum, Tipton Road, Dudley DY1 4SQ

The Canal Museum, Stoke Bruerne, near Towcester, Northamptonshire NN12 7SE

Cotswold Canals Trust Visitor Centre (Stroud), Bell House, Wallbridge Lock, Stroud, Gloucestershire GL5 3JS

Cotswold Canals Trust Visitor Centre (Saul), The Canal Towpath, Church Lane, Saul, Gloucestershire GL2 7LA

Devizes Wharf Kennet & Avon Canal Trust Museum, Couch Lane, Devizes, Wiltshire; SN10 1EB

The Falkirk Wheel, Lime Road, Tamfourhill, Falkirk FK1 4RS

Fourteen Locks Canal Centre, Cwm Lane, Rogerstone, Newport NP10 9GN

Foxton Canal Museum, Middle Lock, Gumley Road, Foxton, Leicestershire LE16 7RA

Gloucester Waterways Museum, Llanthony Warehouse, The Docks, Gloucester GL1 2EH

▲ A preserved narrow boat moored outside the Gloucester Waterways Museum at Gloucester Docks.

▲ The Canal Centre at Linlithgow.

Ironbridge Gorge Museum, Blists Hill Victorian Town, Legges Way, Telford, Shropshire TF7 5DU

Linlithgow Canal Centre, Manse Road Basin, Linlithgow, West Lothian EH49 6AJ

London Canal Museum, 12–13 New Wharf Road, London N1 9RT

National Waterways Museum, South Pier Road, Ellesmere Port, Cheshire CH65 4FW

Standedge Tunnel and Visitor Centre, Waters Road, Marsden, Huddersfield HD7 6NQ

FURTHER INFORMATION

Apart from visiting museums, the best way to get to know the canals is to travel them, either by boat or by walking the towpath. Special points of interest, such as aqueducts, tunnels and flights of locks, are listed by area at www.waterscapes.com.

The Inland Waterways Association is a principal organization for canal enthusiasts and their website provides up-to-date information on what is happening around the country: www.waterways.org.uk.

The Canal and River Trust is a charity responsible for the care of the waterways of England and Wales. There is much information about their work and how to get involved on their website: www.canalrivertrust.org.uk.

Information correct at time of going to press.